5/07

 P9-AFY-156

The Mystery
of Vampires
and
Werewolves

Chris Oxlade

Heinemann Library
Chicago, Illinois

Designed by AMR
Illustrations by Art Construction
Origination by Ambassador Litho Ltd.
Printed in Hong Kong/China

06 05 04 03 02
10 9 8 7 6 5 4 3 2 1

Library of Congress Cataloging-in-Publication Data
  Oxlade, Chris.
  The mystery of vampires and werewolves / Chris Oxlade.
      p. cm. -- (Can science solve?)
  Includes bibliographical references and index.
  Summary: Looks at legends about vampires and werewolves in different
  cultures, their reputed appearance and behavior, similarities between
  the two creatures, and possible scientific explanations of the old
  stories.
   ISBN 1-58810-668-3 (lib. bdg.)   ISBN 1-58810-932-1 (pbk. bdg.)
   1. Vampires. 2. Werewolves. [1. Vampires. 2. Werewolves.] I. Title.

  II. Series.
   BF1556 .O85 2002
   398'.45--dc21
                          2001004541

Acknowledgments
The author and publishers are grateful to the following for permission to reproduce
copyright material:
Corbis/Bettman, p. 4; Fortean Picture Library, pp. 7, 10, 12, 13, 15, 19, 26; Mary Evans
Picture Library, p. 9; Robert Harding Picture Library, p. 11; Science Photo Library, pp. 17,
18, 23, 25; BBC Natural History, pp. 20–21; DK Photos, p. 22; Kobal Collection, p. 27;
Dracula Society, p. 28; Oxford Scientific Films/Richard Packwood, p. 29.

Cover photographs reproduced with permission of Moviestore Collection.

Every effort has been made to contact copyright holders of any material reproduced in
this book. Any omissions will be rectified in subsequent printings if notice is given to
the publisher.

Some words are shown in bold, **like this.** You can find out
what they mean by looking in the glossary.

Contents

About Mysteries

For centuries, people have been puzzled and fascinated by mysterious places, creatures, and events. Is there really a monster in Loch Ness? Did the lost city of Atlantis ever really exist? Are crop circles messages from aliens or simply clever hoaxes? Is there life on Mars or Venus? Do strange creatures such as vampires and werewolves come out at night?

Some of these mysteries have baffled scientists, who have spent years trying to find the answers. But just how far can science go? Can it really explain the unexplained? Are there some mysteries that science simply cannot solve? Read on, and make up your own mind.

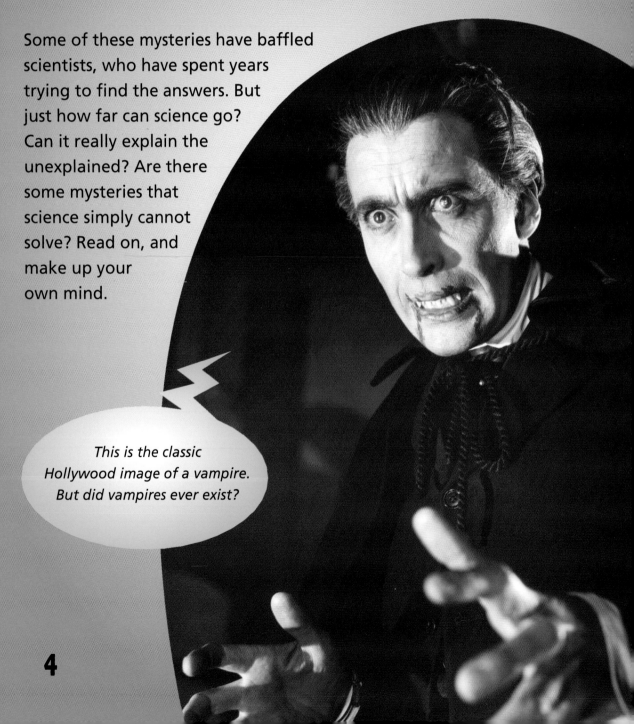

This is the classic Hollywood image of a vampire. But did vampires ever exist?

4

This book tells you about vampires and werewolves. It looks at where the stories about vampires and werewolves come from, what people thought they looked like, some eyewitness accounts of vampires and werewolves, and some theories about what they could really be.

What are vampires?

When you hear the word *vampire,* what do you think of? You probably think of a terrifying, **undead** human figure who goes out at night to find victims and drink their blood. This is what people have believed for hundreds of years. You probably also imagine the figure wearing a long black cape, having two long, sharp fangs, sleeping in a coffin during the day, and turning into a bat at night. Most of these ideas come from novels, films, and television shows about vampires.

What are werewolves?

When you hear the word *werewolf,* what do you think of? Do you think of a person who changes into a wolf, kills and eats people, and then turns back into a human? This is what a **mythical** werewolf is supposed to do. You may have other ideas about werewolves. Perhaps you think that a werewolf looks like a person with a hairy face and hands and has pointy ears and a mouth full of pointy teeth. You have probably gotten these ideas from movies or television.

Most scientists would say that vampires and werewolves are just **myths.** But is there anything science can do to prove whether vampires and werewolves really exist?

Beginnings of a Mystery

It is impossible to tell when and where the first stories about vampires and werewolves were told, but these tales have been around for hundreds, if not thousands, of years. They were originally told in times when most people were religious and very **superstitious,** too. There was no communication such as television and telephones, so people only heard about events by word of mouth. Many stories of strange creatures were passed around.

Home of the vampires

There are stories from all over the world of hideous creatures that sucked blood from their victims. They come from China, North and South America, and Africa. But the most famous stories come from countries in Eastern Europe, such as Hungary, Albania, Romania, and Greece.

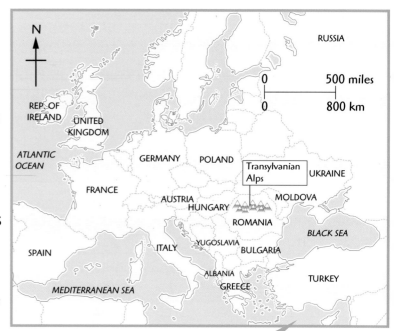

In the **Middle Ages,** the people of Eastern Europe really believed in vampires. Members of the Christian church argued about what vampires were and where they came from. If people thought that there was a vampire around, they dug up graves, searching for people whose bodies had not rotted away.

Many vampire stories come from a region of modern-day Romania called Transylvania.

6

The huge modern-day interest in vampires has come from novels and films made in the last 150 years. This is when the caped, fanged figure we all know appeared. The novel that really started it all was *Dracula*, which was published in 1897.

Ancient werewolves

Some ancient Greek **physicians** believed that certain people could transform themselves into various animal forms. The ancient Greeks and Romans believed that their gods could take many different forms, too. In a Greek **myth,** the king Lycaon was turned into a wolf by the god Zeus. Even in ancient times, Europe was famous for werewolves. Nearly 2,500 years ago, the Greek historian Herodotus wrote about people in central Europe who turned into wolves.

In the Middle Ages, real wolves were much more common than they are today. They killed many people in rural villages. But the villagers often blamed other people for these deaths, claiming that the murderers had turned into wolves to do the deeds.

This is a 16th-century woodcut of a werewolf attack.

What Are Vampires?

Before investigating whether science can help to explain what vampires and werewolves are, we need to know exactly what **myths** about them say. What are they supposed to look like? How are they supposed to act?

The vampire lifestyle

If vampires really exist, what are they? For starters, a vampire is a **supernatural** creature, so it does not obey the laws of physics, chemistry, or biology. In myths, a vampire is a spirit or soul that lives in a dead body. During the day, it sleeps in the grave or coffin where the dead person was buried.

A vampire can only survive by drinking human blood. This gives it life energy or "life force." So, at night, the vampire must leave its coffin or grave and find victims to attack. The human victims cannot defend themselves, because vampires have supernatural strength. A vampire's victim becomes weak and dies from loss of blood. Then he or she becomes a vampire, too.

Not a pretty face

Myths about vampires say that even while in human form, a vampire has recognizable features. Vampires from Eastern Europe, and especially from Transylvania, have very skinny bodies and pale skin. They are said to have eyebrows that meet in the middle, bright, clear eyes that **hypnotize** their victims, pointed **canine** teeth that they use to pierce skin, very red lips, and very nasty breath. They also have long, sharp fingernails and hair on the palms of their hands.

Vampires from other parts of the world are said to have slightly different features. For example, vampires from Mexico are said to have no flesh on their skulls. Vampires from Russia are said to have purple faces.

According to myths, vampires can change shape to take the form of other animals. Usually, they change into bats, but they can also change into wolves. Worse still, they can control other creatures and force them to help with their evil deeds.

This woodcut shows Vlad the Impaler, a legendary vampire from Eastern Europe.

From Person to Wolf

There are many **myths** about what werewolves are supposed to look like and the horrible things they do. Vampires and werewolves have some common features. Like vampires, werewolves are **supernatural** creatures. In the **Middle Ages,** people thought that if a werewolf died, it became a vampire.

A werewolf is a person who can change into a wolf. Usually, the change lasts for just a few hours, but sometimes the change is permanent. When in wolf form, a werewolf hunts human victims, tears out their throats, and eats them. Like vampires, werewolves have supernatural strength when they are in wolf form, so their victims have no hope of escape.

The people of Eschenbach, Germany, hunted a werewolf that terrorized their town in the 17th century.

Mythical werewolves are harmless when they are in human form, though. Some do not even know that they become werewolves. But they are supposed to have strange features, often similar to those of vampires. Like vampires, werewolves have pale skin. Hairiness is another common feature. Werewolves' eyebrows meet in the middle, and their hands and feet are more hairy than normal people's. They also have long, pointy fingernails that are red, like the color of blood. And they have small, pointy ears.

When in wolf form, most mythical werewolves look like real wolves and walk on all fours. The only difference is that they are slightly bigger than real wolves. Some werewolves are said to stand on two legs and have some human features, like the werewolves you see in films. Werewolves in wolf form can still speak and their eyes look like human eyes. Whatever they look like, werewolves are fierce, strong, fast and, most important, very clever.

Do you think this bear could be a person who has changed shapes?

Shape-changing

Werewolves are an example of a mythical creature that can change shape from one animal to another. This ability is called shape-changing, shape-shifting, or morphing. There are many examples of shape-changing supernatural creatures from around the world, such as the man-tigers and man-bears in Asia and man-lizards in New Zealand.

11

Vampire Stories

There are many stories about vampires killing people in local communities. However, there are no reliable eyewitness accounts, either from people who say they have been attacked or from people who say they have seen an attack. There are reports, though, of deaths that appear to have been caused by vampires. Worse still, there are some rather nasty cases of real people killing people in the way that vampires would. These cases must have fueled the vampire **myth**.

Poland, 19th century

In 1870, in the Polish town of Kantrzyno, a man named Franz von Poblocki died of an illness called consumption. He was buried in the local churchyard. Two weeks later, his son, Anton, died of the same illness. Other members of the family fell ill, too. The family believed that Franz must have become a vampire. They decided to stop him before he took any more of their "life blood." With the help of a vampire expert named Dzigielski, they snuck into the churchyard at night, dug up Franz's body, and cut off his head. They were discovered doing the deed and put on trial. In court they claimed that they had acted in self-defense. The judge agreed and let them off!

The Poblocki family was put on trial for digging up their dead father, whom they believed was a vampire.

France, 15th century

Gilles de Rais was a French aristocrat in the 15th century who behaved like a vampire. He was a soldier who fought against the English with the famous female military leader, Joan of Arc. Gilles de Rais was found guilty of murdering 150 people to drink their blood. His servants helped him. He was executed for his crimes in 1440.

Hungary, 17th century

Elizabeth de Bathory was another real person who behaved like a vampire. She was a Polish countess who lived in 17th-century Hungary. Elizabeth liked to bathe in human blood. She believed that it would keep her young. She killed several hundred people to get blood for her baths. She was caught when the authorities broke into her castle. In 1611, she was imprisoned for life. She would have been executed if she had not been a countess.

Was the countess Elizabeth de Bathory a vampire, or just a murderess?

Werewolf Stories

There are eyewitness accounts from people who claimed to have seen werewolves long ago. Just as there are cases of real people acting like vampires, there are cases of people who have acted like werewolves. However, these people were not able to turn into wolves like the werewolves in stories.

Germany, 18th century

In 1721, near the German town of Caasberg, a farmer and his wife were cutting hay in a field with other workers. Suddenly the woman said she could not work anymore and left the field. She told her husband to watch for wild animals and that if an animal came near, he should throw his hat at it and run away. A few minutes later, the farmer spotted a wolf coming toward the field. As instructed, he threw his hat, which distracted the wolf while another man ran behind it and stabbed it with a pitchfork. Instantly, the wolf changed back into human form. To their horror, it was the farmer's wife!

France, 18th century

In 1764, a series of horrible murders and animal killings began in southern France. The murders went on for three years, during which time 40 people were killed and more than 100 others were injured. Survivors said they had been attacked by a huge red creature that had scales and a big mouth full of sharp teeth and could run like the wind. It became known as the Beast of Gevaudan. In 1767, a huge wolf was trapped and killed. The attacks suddenly stopped, but there were still rumors that a werewolf had been responsible.

France, 16th century

Frenchman Jaques Rollet confessed in court that he had used a magic **ointment** to change himself into a wolf. But, he said, he only acted like a wolf. He still looked like a person except for hairy, wolflike hands and feet.

This is an illustration of the legendary Beast of Gevaudan.

Germany, 16th century

Peter Stubbe was an infamous murderer who killed hundreds of people. He was eventually captured and convicted of being a werewolf. It is said that he turned himself into a wolf by putting on a belt made of wolf skin. Stubbe was executed in 1589.

A Dead Person's Soul

There are several theories about what makes a vampire, how to keep people from becoming vampires, and how to kill vampires.

How a vampire is made

According to **myths**, there were many ideas about how people turned into vampires. The most common was that a vampire was the soul of a dead person. The person had died and had been buried, but his or her soul had refused to pass into the spirit world. Instead, it had stayed in this world and used the body of the dead person to do its evil deeds.

There were many **superstitions** about why a person's soul might stay in this world. They included that a person was wicked or was condemned by the church and so could not go to heaven; that he or she was not buried in a proper way; or that he or she committed suicide. Other possibilities were that he or she died a violent death, such as being murdered; or that he or she was a witch or a werewolf. Some people thought that a vampire was the Devil's worker in human form or a person's body taken over by a spirit to do evil. And, of course, any victim of a vampire also became a vampire.

Projections from the mind

*A different **supernatural** theory is that a vampire is something called an **astral projection**. An astral projection is said to be a physical object that is sent out from a person's mind while the person is asleep. Evil spirits or the cruel side of the person's nature take over the projection and make it do evil deeds.*

Stopping a vampire

There were also theories about how to keep people from becoming vampires when they died. One method was to bury a special item, such as a clove of garlic, a lemon, or bread blessed by a priest, along with the body. These methods were supposed to keep the vampire from returning to the body after a night out. Nailing the body into the coffin was also said to work.

Killing vampires required different methods. Hammering a wooden stake, sword, or dagger through a vampire's heart while it slept was said to turn the body to dust. Exposing the vampire to sunlight was also said to kill it.

Carrying a clove of garlic was said to be a good way of keeping vampires away.

Changing into a Wolf

There are several theories about how a werewolf is made and how to kill werewolves.

How a werewolf is made

Different parts of the world have different theories about how an ordinary person can become a werewolf. A person may become a werewolf from sleeping outdoors during a full moon, being born when there is a full moon, drinking water from a stream from which a wolf has drunk, or drinking from a wolf's footprint.

According to **superstition,** there are several ways that a werewolf can turn from human form into wolf form and back again. These include wearing a skin from a real wolf, wearing a belt made of animal skin, or rubbing magic **ointment** on the body. As soon as the skin or ointment is removed, the werewolf returns to human form. Some werewolves can control when they turn from human form into wolf form, others cannot.

Wearing the skin of a real wolf was said to turn a person into wolf form.

In the **Middle Ages,** one theory was that werewolves had skin with hair on the inside. To turn from human to wolf, they simply turned their skin inside out. Many people suspected of being werewolves were killed when angry mobs cut them open to try to find their inward-facing fur.

Identifying a werewolf

According to **myths,** a werewolf can be turned back to human form by saying its human name, by hitting it three times on the forehead, or by making the sign of the cross. Another **supernatural** theory is called wound-doubling. This means that if a werewolf is injured while in wolf form, the wound will still be there when the werewolf turns back to human form. People who claimed to have injured a werewolf would look for a person with the same wound they had caused.

Eliphas Levi believed werewolves were ***astral projections.***

Astral projections

*Some people have a theory about werewolves that is much like one of the theories about vampires: A werewolf who attacks people could be a projection from the mind of a sleeping person. The 19th-century **occultist** Eliphas Levi believed that a person's "sidereal body" could go out into the countryside at night while his or her physical body was asleep, dreaming about being a wolf.*

The Vampire Disease

There is one theory about vampires that is based on science. Some doctors now think that people who were thought to be vampires in fact had terrible diseases. This theory does not explain how **mythical** vampires could exist, but it does explain how some vampire stories might have started.

Mixed-up genes

Genes are the units of hereditary information in each cell of your body that control how your body grows and the job that each cell does. They are passed on from generation to generation. Sometimes people are born with small mistakes in their genes, which are called mutations. Some mutations cause diseases.

One rare disease caused by a mutation is *erythropoietic porphyria.* This disease was common in noble families of Eastern Europe in the **Middle Ages.** It makes the skin, eyes, and teeth look red and makes the upper lip pull back, revealing the teeth. If sufferers go out in the sun, their lips and skin crack and bleed. *Erythropoietic porphyria* was not identified as a disease until the 19th century, so doctors in the Middle Ages did not know how to treat it. They locked the patient in a dark place during day to reduce the bleeding and only let him or her out at night. The sufferer was also made to drink blood to replace what was lost through bleeding. Sadly, the disease was usually fatal.

These are the forests of Transylvania, where the disease erythropoietic porphyria *was common.*

You can imagine the rumors that spread about these strange-looking children who had red eyes, whose top teeth showed, who drank blood, and who only came out at night.

Did vampires have rabies?

*Rabies is a disease caused by a **virus**. It is spread when an infected animal bites another animal. Among the animals that can get rabies are dogs, bats, and humans. Rabies makes people so aggressive that they sometimes try to bite. It makes it hard to sleep, so people with rabies are awake at night. Rabies also makes people sensitive to things such as bright lights and smells. And it causes facial muscles to tense up, making the lips curl back in a snarl. Perhaps people with rabies were mistaken for vampires in the past. There is evidence of a serious rabies outbreak in Hungary in the 1720s, when many vampire stories began.*

Animal Vampires

Drinking blood may be a horrible way to live, but it is not as strange as it seems. The only real vampires that we know exist today are not humans. They are animals. There are several animals that feed on blood, including insects, leeches, and the famous vampire bat. The feeding habits of these animals may have led to stories about vampires turning into bat form at night.

Vampire bats

The vampire bat lives in Central and South America. Like other bats, it is a **mammal.** It is the only mammal that lives on blood. The vampire bat is quite small, not much bigger than a mouse. It searches for sleeping animals with the use of **echolocation.** Once the bat finds a victim, it drinks its blood. Its victims include large animals, such as cows and sheep.

Because of its name and its two long, sharp teeth, people often think the vampire bat uses its fangs like a **mythical** vampire to suck blood. In fact, the vampire bat does not use its teeth that way, and it does not kill its victims.

Here you can see the sharp teeth of a vampire bat.

22

It actually uses its sharp front teeth to cut a tiny piece of skin from its victim. Then, for a few minutes, it drinks the blood that oozes from the wound. The bat's saliva contains a chemical that keeps the blood from clotting while the bat is drinking it. None of this harms the host animal. The sleeping victim often never knows that a bat has enjoyed its blood. Vampire bats sometimes drink so much blood that they are too heavy to fly until the meal is digested.

Insect blood-suckers

Many kinds of insects live on the blood of mammals and birds. They are called **parasitic** insects. They include fleas, mosquitoes, and **midges.** These insects feed by sticking their sharp mouthparts into the skin of their victim to find small blood vessels near the surface, called capillaries. Then they suck out the blood through a narrow tube.

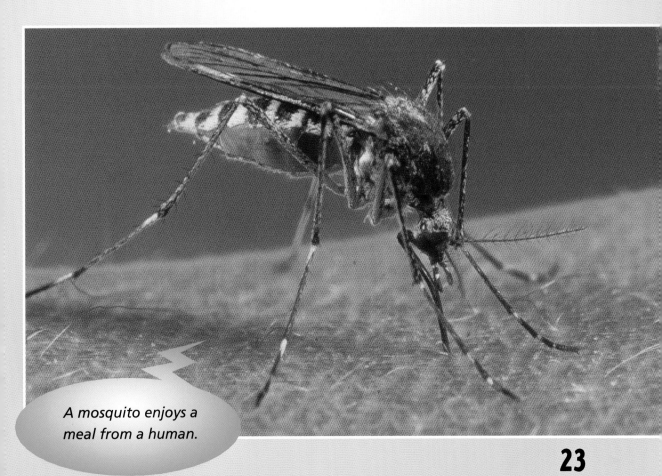

A mosquito enjoys a meal from a human.

Werewolf Science

At the moment, science cannot explain how humans could turn into wolves. But there is one scientific theory about werewolves that may explain where the **myths** about them came from. As with vampires, the theory is a medical one.

Lycanthropy

The word *lycanthrope* comes from the Greek words *lycos*, which means "wolf," and *anthropos*, which means "man." So *lycanthrope* means "wolf-man." In ancient Greece, the word referred to someone who had turned into a beast.

Today, the words *werewolf* and *lycanthrope* are sometimes used to mean the same thing, but they have different meanings. A **mythical** werewolf is someone who is said to have physically transformed into a wolf by some magical or **supernatural** power, whereas a lycanthrope only believes he or she has changed into a wolf.

A lycanthrope suffers from a mental illness called lycanthropy. A person suffering from lycanthropy imagines that he or she looks and behaves like a wolf. In reality, however, the sufferer has not changed in appearance in any way. Lycanthropes often say that they have their wolf fur on the inside of their skin, which is why they look human. **Psychiatrists** call lycanthropy a form of delusion. The illness was first seen in the 7th century, when sufferers were described as moving on four legs and howling at night.

Brain poisoning

Another theory about werewolf stories comes from the **Middle Ages.** Poor people often suffered from dreamlike **hallucinations** that are thought to have been caused by eating damp grain. The damp grain often had a type of **fungus,** called claviceps, growing on it. It is known as **ergotized** grain.

This fungus makes a chemical called lysergic acid diethylamide (LSD). We now know that if taken in large doses, this chemical can cause people to think a lot of strange things. They might even think they are turning into an animal. How many peasants thought they were turning into wolves because of eating damp grain?

Ergotized grain can cause hallucinations. Can this explain beliefs about werewolves?

Stories and Films

The **mythical** stories of vampires and werewolves are both fascinating and scary. It is no wonder that so many novels have been written about them, and dozens of films and popular television shows have been made about them.

Dracula

The first vampire and werewolf novels were written in the 19th century, when horror stories became popular. One of the first was *Varney the Vampire; or, The Feast of Blood,* published in 1847. But most famous of all was *Dracula,* the novel that became the inspiration for many films. *Dracula* was written by an Irish novelist named Bram Stoker and published in 1897.

In the novel, Count Dracula travels to England to find victims. He is hunted down by the fiancée of one of the women he attacks, along with a vampire expert. They eventually follow Dracula to his castle in Transylvania and kill him.

This portrait of Count Dracula comes from a castle in Austria.

The vampire in the story, Count Dracula, was based on a real person who lived in the 15th century. His name was Vlad Tepes. He became Prince Vlad the Fourth of Wallachia, an area in modern-day Romania. Vlad was a **tyrant** in his own country and apparently killed about 40,000 enemy prisoners of war by impaling them on sharp sticks. This was how he earned one of his nicknames—Vlad the Impaler. His other nickname was Romanian for "son of the Devil" or "son of the dragon"—*Draculaea.* Dracula's castle was probably modeled after the Csejthe, the castle of Elizabeth de Bathory, the woman who bathed in blood.

People are still fascinated by the idea of werewolves. This one is from the 1981 film An American Werewolf in London.

Werewolf tales

There also have been novels and films about werewolves. One of the earliest stories was *William and the Werewolf,* written in France in the late 12th century. Films include Hammer Horror's *Curse of the Werewolf* (1960). Stories about other shape-changing creatures are also popular, especially in superhero comic stories.

In Conclusion

Can science really solve the mystery of vampires and werewolves? What is certain is that, at the moment, science cannot support the **myths** of vampires or werewolves. It cannot explain how a spirit could take over a body, as a vampire is said to do. Neither can it explain how a human could change shapes, transforming into a wolf as a werewolf is said to do.

Scientists tend to dismiss eyewitness accounts of vampires and werewolves, because they mostly come from so long ago, when people knew little about science and medicine. The scientists' argument is made stronger because there are hardly any cases of people seeing real vampires or werewolves. There is just no reliable evidence for them. On the other hand, some eyewitness accounts can be explained by the medical theories.

There is no doubt that some people in the past were convinced that vampires and werewolves existed—and that they were very scared of them. Some people still believe in them.

This is the logo of the modern Dracula Society.

CREDO QUIA IMPOSSIBLE

Now that you have read about vampires and werewolves and the possible explanations for them, can you draw any conclusions? Do you feel that you can dismiss any of the theories without investigating them further, even though some have no evidence to support them? Do you believe that **supernatural** creatures such as vampires and werewolves could exist? Or do you only believe things that science can prove? Do you have any theories of your own?

What do you think?

Can we accept evidence of vampires and werewolves from hundreds of years ago that may have been passed on by word of mouth before being written down? Do you think the myths continue because they are fascinating and scary? Will you keep an eye out for people with red eyes, pointy fingernails, and hairy hands?

This looks like a perfect night for vampires and werewolves!

Try to keep an open mind. Remember that if scientists throughout history had not bothered to investigate things that appeared to be strange or mysterious, many scientific discoveries may never have been made.

Glossary

astral projection   physical object or being that is sent out from a person's mind in some way

canine   describes anything to do with the dog family (including wolves). Canine teeth are the extra-long, pointed teeth on either side of a dog's jaw.

delusion   false belief or opinion

echolocation   way of finding the position of an object by sending out sounds and listening for any echoes that bounce off objects. Bats use echolocation to find their way and to hunt for food.

ergotized   describes grain that has a particular type of fungus growing on it

fungus   organism that is not an animal or plant and that lives on decaying plants or animals. Mushrooms, toadstools, and molds are all fungi.

hallucination   something that you think you hear or see, but that does not really exist

hypnotize   put a person into a sleeplike state in which they obey commands and answer questions

mammal   warm-blooded animal that has a backbone and feeds milk to its young

Middle Ages   name given to the period in European history from about 1000 to about 1450

midge   certain kind of fly

myth   traditional story or common idea or belief that is false

mythical   describes something, such as a werewolf, that appears in myths

occultist   person who believes in and studies supernatural events

ointment   cream that is rubbed onto the skin

parasitic describes an organism that lives and feeds on another organism

physician doctor or healer

psychiatrist doctor who studies and treats mental diseases

supernatural creature or event that cannot be explained by the science that we understand today

superstition belief in something supernatural

superstitious describes a person who believes in superstitions

tyrant someone who is an oppressive or cruel ruler

undead describes a supernatural being that lives in the body of a dead person

virus microorganism that brings disease. Viruses can only be seen through a microscope.

Further Reading

Oxlade, Chris. *The Mystery of Haunted Houses.* Chicago: Heinemann Library, 1999.

Oxlade, Chris. *The Mystery of Life on Other Planets.* Chicago: Heinemann Library, 2002.

Wallace, Holly. *The Mystery of the Abominable Snowman.* Chicago: Heinemann Library, 1999.

Wallace, Holly. *The Mystery of the Loch Ness Monster.* Chicago: Heinemann Library, 1999.

Index